My Favorite Foods

by Al Woodsen

HOUGHTON MIFFLIN HARCOURT
School Publishers

PHOTOGRAPHY CREDITS: Cover © UpperCut Images/Alamy; 1 © Thinkstock/Jupiterimages; 2 © UpperCut Images/ Alamy; 3 © SuperStock/Alamy; 4 © Digital Vision/Alamy, (inset) © Runk/Schoenberger/Alamy; 5 © Westend61/Alamy; 6 © Radius Images/Jupiterimages; 7 © Thinkstock/Jupiterimages; 8 © Dennis MacDonald/Alamy; 9 © Chris Pancewicz/Alamy; 10 © Jupiterimages/Able Stock/Alamy

Printed in China

ISBN-13: 978-0-547-42741-6
ISBN-10: 0-547-42741-7

7 8 9 10 0940 18 17 16 15 14 13
4500396742

garden

This is my garden.
Some of my favorite
food grows here.

tomatoes

These are tomatoes.
They grow on a vine.

carrots

These are carrots.
They grow
under the ground.

beans

These are beans.
They grow on a plant.

corn

This is corn.
It grows on
a very tall plant.

apples

Apples are fruit.
Sometimes you can pick
them right off the tree.

7

cherries

Cherries are fruit.
You can make cherry pie.
First you have to pick
a lot of cherries!

8

berries

These are berries.
Berries are fruit, too.
They grow on bushes.

These are my
favorite foods.
What are your
favorite foods?

Responding

✔ **WORDS TO KNOW** Word Builder

What kinds of food grow in a garden?

Write About It

Text to Self What is your favorite food? Draw a picture. Write a sentence to tell about your picture.

✔ **WORDS TO KNOW**

first	**sometimes**
food	**these**
ground	**under**
right	**your**

✔ **TARGET STRATEGY** Summarize

Stop to tell important ideas as you read.